THE NIGHT BEFORE CHRISTMAS

THE NIGHT BEFORE CHRISTMAS

by CLEMENT CLARKE MOORE

Illustrated by
TASHA TUDOR

Rand McNally & Company

Library of Congress Cataloging in Publication Data

Moore, Clement Clarke, 1779-1863.
  The night before Christmas.

  SUMMARY: The well-known poem about an important
Christmas Eve visitor.
  [1. Christmas poetry] I. Tudor, Tasha. II. Ti-
tle.
PZ8.3.M782N65   811′.2   75-8858
ISBN 0-528-82181-4
ISBN 0-528-80144-9 lib. bdg.

First printing, 1975
Second printing, 1976
Third printing, 1976
Fourth printing, 1978
Fifth printing, 1979
Sixth printing, 1980
Seventh printing, 1982
Eighth printing, 1983

The Night
Before Christmas

'Twas the night before Christmas,
when all through the house

Not a creature was stirring,
not even a mouse.

The stockings were hung
by the chimney with care,

In hopes that St. Nicholas

soon would be there.

The children were nestled
all snug in their beds,

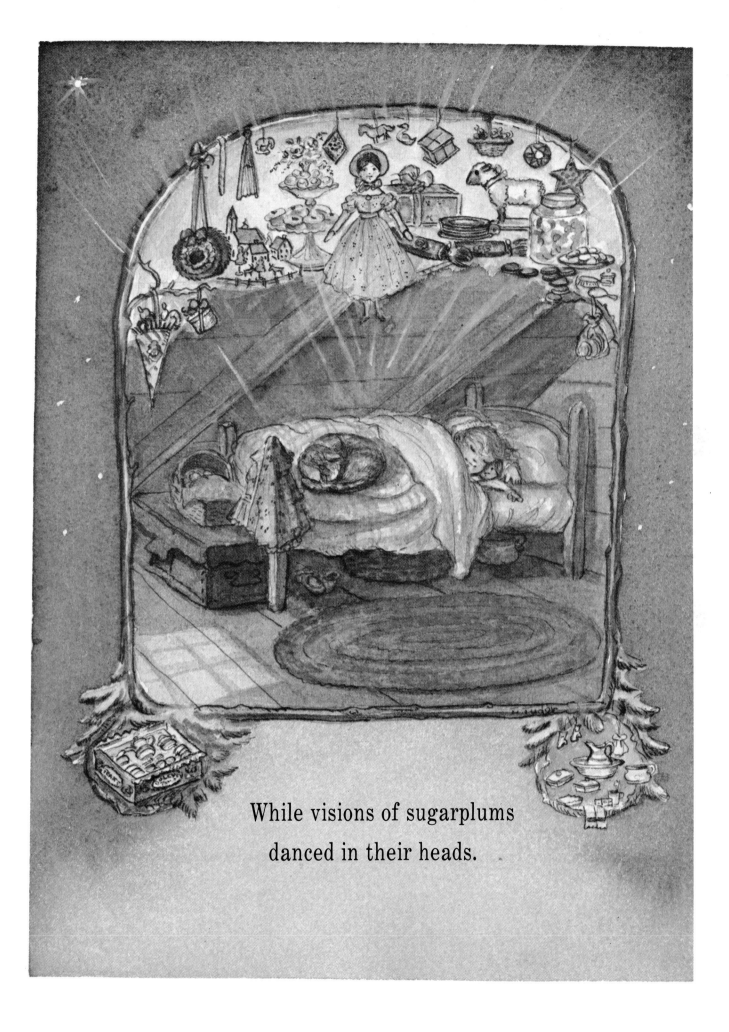

While visions of sugarplums
danced in their heads.

And Mamma in her kerchief
and I in my cap

Had just settled our brains
for a long winter's nap,

When out on the lawn

there arose such a clatter,

I sprang from my bed

to see what was the matter.

Away to the window
I flew like a flash,

Tore open the shutters
and threw up the sash.

The moon on the breast
of the new-fallen snow
Gave the luster of midday
to objects below,

When what to my wondering
eyes should appear,
But a miniature sleigh
and eight tiny reindeer,

With a little old driver
so lively and quick,

I knew in a moment
it must be St. Nick.

More rapid than eagles
his coursers they came,
And he whistled and shouted
and called them by name:

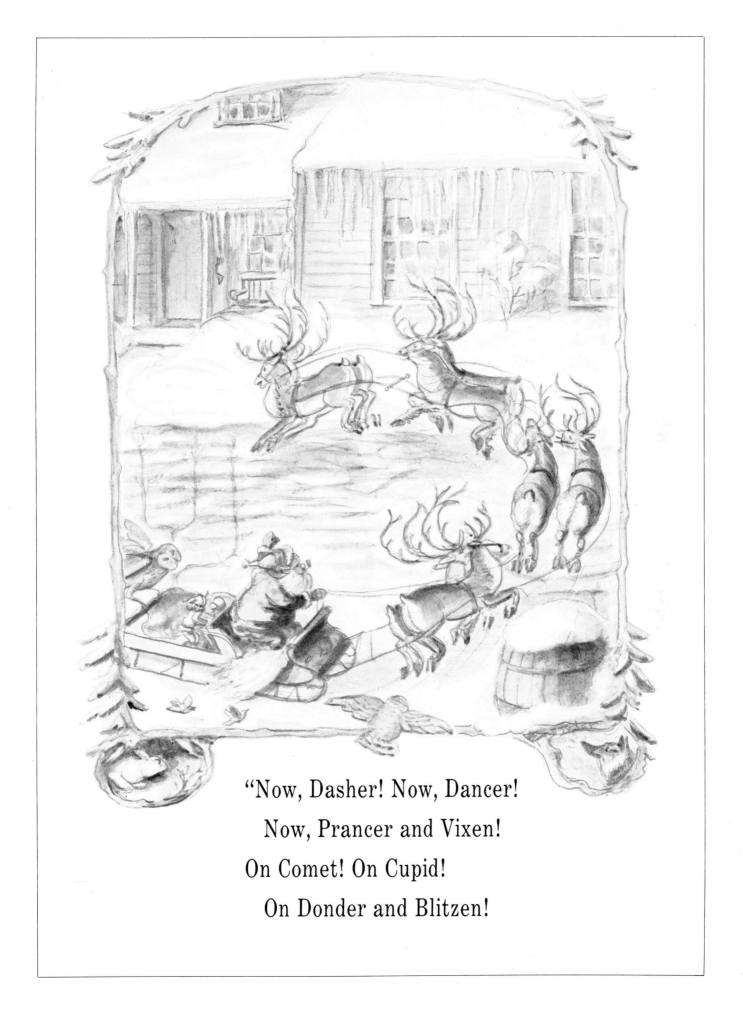

"Now, Dasher! Now, Dancer!
Now, Prancer and Vixen!
On Comet! On Cupid!
On Donder and Blitzen!

To the top of the porch,
to the top of the wall!

Now dash away! Dash away!
Dash away all!"

As dry leaves that before
   the wild hurricane fly
When they meet with an obstacle,
   mount to the sky,

So up to the housetop
the coursers they flew,
With the sleigh full of toys,
and St. Nicholas too.

And then, in a twinkling,

I heard on the roof

The prancing and pawing

of each little hoof.

As I drew in my head
and was turning around,
Down the chimney St. Nicholas
came with a bound.

He was dressed all in fur
from his head to his foot,

And his clothes were all tarnished
with ashes and soot.

A bundle of toys

he had flung on his back,

And he looked like a peddler
just opening his pack.

His eyes, how they twinkled!
His dimples, how merry!

His cheeks were like roses,
his nose like a cherry!

His droll little mouth

was drawn up like a bow,

And the beard on his chin
was as white as the snow.

The stump of a pipe
he held tight in his teeth,

And the smoke it encircled
his head like a wreath.

He had a broad face

and a little round belly

That shook when he laughed

like a bowl full of jelly.

He was chubby and plump,
   a right jolly old elf,
And I laughed when I saw him,
   in spite of myself.

A wink of his eye
and a twist of his head
Soon gave me to know
I had nothing to dread.

He spoke not a word
    but went straight to his work
And filled all the stockings,
    then turned with a jerk,

And laying his finger
aside of his nose,
And giving a nod,
up the chimney he rose.

He sprang to his sleigh,

to his team gave a whistle,

And away they all flew

like the down of a thistle.

But I heard him exclaim
ere he drove out of sight,

"Happy Christmas to all
and to all a good night!"

The Author
and the Illustrator

It was the day before Christmas, a day turned cold and crystalline. The professor, who had just returned from a visit to the market in nearby New York town, warmed himself at the fire in his study and toyed with an amusing idea that had tumbled into his mind during the sleigh ride home. Sounds drifted into the room. The excited scamperings of children's feet. Whispers. Hushed giggles. The professor smiled, picked up his pen, and began to write as poets do, deleting a word here, inserting one there, quickening a phrase, bettering a rhyme. As he worked, the poem came vibrantly alive. "'Twas the night before Christmas, / when all through the house . . ." Several hours later he emerged from his study, his Christmas gift to his children complete. He had, in that brief time, unknowingly changed the future aspect of Christmas celebrations for all American children to come.

The idea of Santa Claus had existed throughout the Western world for many hundreds of years. He appeared in numerous forms. In Germany he was Kris Kringle. In Holland he was St. Nicholas. The Santa Claus given life in the comfortable country household in New York that long ago Christmas Eve was essentially the one we know today, "a right jolly old elf," bearded, twinkling eyed, broad of face, with "a little round belly / that shook when he laughed / like a bowl full of jelly." This Santa was magical. An elf who flew through the sky in an airborne sleigh drawn by not one but eight reindeer with delightfully improbable names. A fairy creature who slid down chimneys and when ready to leave simply lay his finger aside of his nose and "giving a nod up the chimney he rose."

The year was 1822. Clement Clarke Moore was the professor. Born July 15, 1779, in New York, he had graduated from Columbia College and was a professor of religion. At least one of his scholarly works had already appeared in print, and more were to follow. But it is for the imaginative, light-hearted Christmas poem for children that he is remembered.

It is believed Moore never meant his poem for any audience other than his children—whether because he thought so light-hearted a vision of Christmas beneath the dignity of a serious scholar, or because he dismissed the poem as a trivial amusement, is open to speculation. Whatever his reason, the poem was printed anonymously. It appeared without credit in 1823 in the Troy *Sentinel*—given to the paper, it is thought, by a family friend—and was widely reprinted thereafter as "An Account of a Visit from St. Nicholas." The poem remained unacknowledged until 1837 when it was included in an anthology of poetry along with several other poems by Moore.

"The Night Before Christmas," as the poem is now known, first appeared in book form in 1848, decorated with the austere line drawings of T. C. Boyd. Many artists thereafter illustrated the poem. The most famous of the old illustrations were created for *Harpers Weekly* during the 1860s by Thomas Nast, the political cartoonist who is also responsible for the Republican elephant and the Democratic donkey. It was Thomas Nast who first dressed Santa in red fur trimmed with white and belted in black, the unmistakable costume of today.

Tasha Tudor, illustrator of this edition, is famed for the delicacy of her watercolors and for the quaintness of her period settings. Details in her illustrations reach straight to the heart of childhood to appeal to children of any era. Outdoors, owls and chipmunks and flying squirrels lead Santa and his reindeer to a safe rooftop landing. Indoors, a cat and a corgi make him welcome. A doll dances. A clown turns cartwheels. The corgi dons Santa's cap and puffs on his pipe. And under the floor—as every child knows there must be—is an amusing and complete miniature house for a mouse.

Miss Tudor has given us a highly personalized version of "The Night Before Christmas." The house, inside and out, is her own Vermont farm home designed in exact detail after one of 1740. Inside are to be found the rocking horse and the doll carriage shown on the endpapers at the front of the book, the doll that peeks from Santa's pack—"possessor of an extensive wardrobe"—and the Noah's ark. The ornaments on the Christmas tree date to the 1840s and once belonged to Miss Tudor's grandmother. And naturally, in residence in the house are a corgi and a cat.

A hundred and fifty years separate the author, Clement Clarke Moore, and the illustrator, Tasha Tudor. Their talents span the years and join to give today's children a delightfully whimsical Christmas treat.